Personal Branding Secrets For 2019

Next Level Strategies to Brand Yourself Online through Instagram, YouTube, Twitter, and Facebook And Why Digital, Network, and Social Media Marketing is King

Written by Gary Ramsey

an illegal act irrespective of if it is done electronically or in print. This extends to creating a secondary or tertiary copy of the work or a recorded copy and is only allowed with an expressed written consent from the Publisher. All additional rights reserved.

The information in the following pages is broadly considered to be a truthful and accurate account of facts and as such any inattention, use or misuse of the information in question by the reader will render any resulting actions solely under their purview. There are no scenarios in which the publisher or the original author of this work can be in any fashion deemed liable for any hardship or damages that may befall them after undertaking information described herein.

Additionally, the information in the following pages is intended only for informational purposes and should thus be thought of as universal. As befitting its nature, it is presented without assurance regarding its prolonged validity or interim quality. Trademarks that are mentioned are done without written consent and can in no way be considered an endorsement from the trademark holder.

Table of Contents

Introduction

Congratulations on purchasing your own copy of *Personal Branding Secrets*!

This book was curated for those who are looking to build personal brands and watch them flourish in 2019. Whether you already have a personal brand started or you are looking to start one, this book will include plenty of information to help you develop a strong foundation and move forward with great strength. The strategies in this book are focused on the key social media platforms for 2019: Facebook, Instagram, Twitter, and YouTube. These platforms are essential in any personal brand that is looking to maximize exposure, gain followers, and increase engagement in a way that will win over conversions and support them in creating great success in the year to come.

Personal branding is a form of branding that highlights you, the person, as the brand.

Personal brands are built for many reasons and represent many different companies. For example, solo musicians, entrepreneurs, influencers, politicians, and other similar one-person-based companies are all considered to be built around personal brands. In fact, you can probably identify many personal brands off the top of your head: Jay-Z, Ree Drummond from The Pioneer Woman blog, Gary Vee, and Oprah Winfrey are all popular personal brands. Building a personal brand is a powerful tool that can support you in setting yourself up for personal success in your career or business.

Knowing how to brand yourself effectively is the key to creating the success you desire. Going into 2019, many new trends are arising that are supporting individuals in having stronger personal brands. The way that brands connect, share, and engage with their audience is changing entirely. The social media empires are rapidly adjusting their focus to become more social than ever since introducing the concept of running online businesses through them. In the past, cold messaging, having an image without much engagement, and accumulating likes and followers was the focus of most brands online. Nowadays, everything is changing. People want to follow other people, *real* people with personalities, compassion, empathy, consideration, and manners. People are interested in following those with purpose, passion, and values. They want to create relationships with the people they are supporting, not just feel like they are another number on their mark of success.

If you want to build a successful personal brand in 2019, you are going to need to know how to create a brand that supports the needs of your followers. That includes knowing how to effectively socialize with them in a way that shows them you care and appreciate their support. You also need to know how to serve them. This can all be done by taking advantage of the many features of the online space and growing your personal brand through social media using the latest and greatest strategies. If you enforce the strategies and concepts within this book consistently throughout 2019, one thing is for sure: you will become *known*.

Chapter 1:
What is Branding

I want to introduce this concept assuming that you know what a brand is. A brand put simply, is a company's image. It is their name. When I say Coca-Cola, L'Oreal, or Build A Bear Workshop, it is likely that you know exactly what it is that I am talking about. You probably even have an image come to your mind that represents whom I am talking about. This is because these are strong *brands*.

But what is *branding* exactly? Well, that answer is just as simple and yet, slightly more complex. Imagine you are walking down the street and you see a golden-yellow colored "M." What would you likely think about? The answer is probably "McDonald's." Why? Because McDonald's is famous for their golden arches. This is just the same as Chevy is famous for their "+" shaped emblem, Ford is famous for their namesake emblem, Sephora is famous for their white and black striping, Wal-Mart is famous for their blue vests, and Pepsi is famous for their electric blue coloring. When you see something that immediately makes you think of a specific company, you are experiencing branding.

Branding is the process of creating a mental resonance between you and your image. It is comprised of a symbol, a design, a name, a sound, a reputation, a series of emotions, employees, your tone, and so much more. The entire package, known as a branding package, is specifically designed to create a "character" for your company. Branding, then, is building a relationship between that "character" and your audience.

Ever since marketing became a thing, branding was an essential element of the business. Companies designed brands as a way to make their name memorable, tangible, and identifiable. The idea was that if your brand could easily be identified and remembered, your audience would remember you and would be more likely to purchase from you. It is likely that this was just a basic idea in the beginning, but branding has gone on to represent a powerful psychological reaction that happens in people. Think about it: when you see a bright metallic red background with a hatless Santa Claus on top of it, you probably think of Coca Cola's annual and traditional Christmas campaign, right? This is because of branding. This psychological reaction that causes you to recall a brand, even if it was not triggered by something that brand put out for you to see, is something that branding relies on. It is the same as remembering your friend Frank every time you see frogs because you know he likes frogs, or remembering a specific memory with your mother every time you make a turkey at Thanksgiving because that was a fond memory the two of you shared. The psychological reaction, then, is the same as you have a relationship with the brand. It is powerful, it is emotionally charged, and it creates a deep attachment that creates meaning for you. The brand becomes important to you.

Branding is not just an age-old practice that businesses continue to use just because it is commonplace, however. Now more than ever, branding is essential. In a world where many businesses are largely building themselves online, branding is a way to stand out from the rest of the businesses that you are surrounded by. At one time, your only competition would be those in the local vicinity. A pet store would compete with the other local pet store unless they were far enough apart that they both accounted for two separate regions of the same locale. Nowadays, your competition is every single other company in the world that is selling the same thing that you are. You are a part of a global market, meaning that you need to know how to brand so that you can develop global relationships and be widely known by your target audience.

Going into 2019, branding is going to be one of the most important aspects of any single business to exist. Without proper and effective branding, someone else who has created a more memorable image is going to rapidly come in and take over your audience, leaving you in the dust. Rather than being the one getting hijacked, you need to be the one building your audience and creating successful relationships for yourself between you and your followers and customers.

Beyond branding your business, you are going to need to brand *yourself*. This is not just true for those who are actually running a personal brand, either. This is true for anyone. You *are* the face of your company, whether it is self-titled based around you or not. This means that you need to brand yourself in a way that positively represents your company and yourself so that you can maximize your success in the online business world in 2019. In this book, you are going to learn just how to do that.

Chapter 2:
Introducing Personal
Branding in 2019

Personal branding gives you the opportunity to get better jobs or better gigs, earn more clients or sales through your business, get industry recognition, create new opportunities for yourself or your company, and more. Going forward in 2019, personal branding is going to be essential for anyone who is interested in developing any level of success in their lives, whether it is on a personal level or within their business.

The key differences of personal branding in 2019 will be based around how networking is done. In the past, individuals could build a reputation for themselves or their personal brands by networking at business meetings, socials, and gatherings. Many would attend dinners, charity events, and other networking socials to meet other business-minded folk and build a reputation for them that allowed them to become recognized and well-known for who they were. While these aspects have not changed, the online front has given individuals a much wider platform to work with. Now, personal brands can be managed online through the same key skills: networking and socializing.

The more you focus on networking in 2019, the better your brand is going to grow. Whether you are building your reputation to support you in getting a better career, or you want to increase your exposure to maximize your personal business, having a strong networking strategy in 2019 is going to support you in becoming more easily recognized by your desired audience.

Networking on social media seems simple enough: you create an account, you post a few times, and you get comments, right? Wrong. Social media is rapidly evolving and the networking front needs to be done with far more intimate strategies now. If you want to have a strong reputation built on social media, you need to be incorporating many different styles of sharing, engaging, and interacting with your audience. This means taking advantage of the many different features available on social media platforms, as well as spreading out and covering multiple different platforms. The more you spread out and the more you engage, the more you will become known by your audience. This is how you will create a reputation, build relationships, and maximize your success in 2019.

If you truly want to create your mark of success in today's world, you need to know how to stand out from the rest of the crowd. With virtually everyone being exposed to a global markets' worth of faces and profiles, standing out is the only way to be recognized, stay fresh and relevant, and be seen by your desired audience. Doing so is not nearly as hard as you would think, though it does require you to understand how social media works, recognize the importance of the social aspect, and consistency. If you incorporate the many strategies shared within this book then you can guarantee one thing, your social media strategy for your personal brand will be strong and your capacity to become recognized by your desired audience and stay relevant will be inevitable.

In 2019, the competition is getting fiercer, but the strategies are evolving as well. With social media being around for more than 10 years now, people and businesses alike are well aware of how social media can be leveraged. As we shift into a more digitized world, taking advantage of this leverage can only mean great results for you.

Chapter 3:
Building A Personal Brand

Building your personal brand will require three primary things: a vision, a strategy, and motivation. As long as you know exactly what you are creating, you have a strong strategy to create it, and you are motivated to the cause, you can create a powerful personal brand that will be recognizable and admirable.

The thing about personal brands is that they are not just business-oriented, they are *personal*. This means that your personal brand needs to be integrated into your own vision for your own life, as the two will be one and the same in the long-run. That being said, the rest of this chapter is going to support you in understanding how you can build your personal vision and what will be required to support you in designing your personal core strategy. We will also explore what will motivate you to keep you focused and on track so that you can have a strong foundation to support you in going forward.

Building Your Vision

The first step to building your personal brand is building your vision. For a standard business model, one would create a mission statement, outline their values, and determine what their overall vision was. This vision would be designed to incorporate their idea of where they would be 1, 2, 5, and 10+ years down the road. Doing the same for your personal brand is a must, as this gives you a clear direction to move in. When you know where you are going, creating your strategy and taking action is much easier.

Building your vision for your personal brand ultimately requires you to determine how you want your life to look. Since this is your personal brand, you need to look at it from a personal point of view. Consider what you want all aspects of your life to look like and how your brand fits into that. For example, if you want to travel a lot and running a travel company is your ideal brand, then you can clearly see that these two will work well together, and you can design your entire brand around travel. If you are more of a homebody and you love creating products or services, you can pick your favorite types of products or services to create and brand yourself in that particular field. Ultimately, your vision and your brand need to coincide.

When you know what you want for yourself and what your top priorities are in life for both now and later in the future, it becomes easier to brand yourself. For this part, there are no right or wrong answers. All you are doing is creating a vision and determining what you truly like the most about that vision.

To build your vision, follow the steps below. This will help you understand who you are, what you want, and what you are working toward in life.

Determine and Prioritize Your Values

Before you can identify what your personal brand is, you need to know what your values are. This is how you can determine what matters to you and how things need to look in order for you to truly feel satisfied in your life. Many people will overlook their true values and dream up a life fed to them by society. As a result, they may find themselves struggling to stay committed to anything or feeling like an imposter in their own life because they are living out of alignment with their values. Staying clear on and true to your values will do you a world of wonders in your life. Not only does it keep you feeling aligned and focused, but it also gives those paying attention to your brand a clear and authentic understanding of what matters to you. Believe it or not, if you attempt to work against your values, this discrepancy will be picked up on by many and it can take away from your reputation. Our values are things we are generally very focused on, concerned with, and passionate about so it can be very clear when we are not living in alignment with them.

Your values are the things that matter most in your life. Values often revolve around family, friends, community, ambitions, intelligence and knowledge, charity, important causes, and other such things. In essence, your values are anything that you regard in high value and feel are important in your life. These are the things that you consider "deal breakers" in your life. For example, say you hold family and – in particular – quality time with your family to high importance. It is likely that you would not want to take a career that pulls you away from having quality time with your family on a regular basis. Our values determine what we want for ourselves as they help us discover what means the most to us and how we can structure our lives to honor those things.

Many people feel that having strong and honorable values is important. While it certainly is, it is also important that your values are true to you. For that reason, refrain from adding any values to your list that you do not personally feel attached to. These will muddy your list, take away from what you truly care about, and prevent you from staying motivated to your vision because your vision will ultimately be built on something that is meaningless to you.

Once you have determined what all of your values are, you need to prioritize them based on what is the most important to you. Knowing what your core values are (the ones that are most important to you) versus your other values is important. Your core values will be the first to be considered whenever you are making important decisions in your life. The rest will come into play, but not necessarily as "deal breakers."

Identify What Your Passions Are

Now, with a clear understanding of what your values are, you also need to identify your passions. Your passions are comprised of virtually anything that you love doing the most. These may overlap with your values, but they should also be different. Not all will overlap, and that is okay. Typically, your values will be more broad (i.e. "family"), but your passions will be more specific (i.e. "taking your family on vacations.") Passions should not just be interests, but things that you genuinely like doing and that you can stay committed to.

You should outline two sets of passions: personal passions and professional passions. Your personal passions should be everything you love doing in your personal time that helps you feel more fulfilled. Your professional passions should be the things that you love doing that have the capacity to add to your career or entrepreneurial pursuit.

When it comes to personal branding, you will want to talk about both types of passions. However, your professional passions should naturally be the predominantly discussed passions. This will not take away from your personal passions, but it will help you identify yourself based on a professional nature. Your personal passions can then be shared and discussed in a way that adds to the many layers of who you are and gives you depth for those who enjoy following you and interacting with you in the online space.

Determine Your Ideal Traits

Your next step in envisioning your personal brand is identifying what your traits are. Understanding what makes you who you are and recognizing what your key traits and characteristics help you to identify yourself. If you can easily identify yourself in a describable manner, then identifying yourself to others will be infinitely easier. Furthermore, you can choose to create a vision that compliments your traits, rather than attempt to create and commit to one that is completely misaligned for who you are.

You should ideally be outlining both your best traits and your flaws. This can help you understand what your strengths and weaknesses are, helping to guide you forward on your journey of understanding yourself and building your vision.

The traits that you incorporate in your outline should be measured. In other words, put them on a scale of 1-to-10, where 1 means you have that trait but only a small amount, and 10 means you have that trait to the maximum degree. This can help you understand who you are in a more accurate manner and help you determine whether your vision will actually fit with you or not.

Discuss With Those Closest to You

The last step in discovering who you are is talking with the people who are closest to you. Asking loved ones or close friends what they think of you and how they honestly identify you is a great way to discover how other people already see you. This means that you can verify if who you are and who you want to be or brand yourself as are aligned or not. Furthermore, it will support you in discovering how you can make the necessary adjustments to get to where you want to go.

Putting it All Together

Now that you have a clear understanding of who you are, what you value, and what you are passionate about, creating your vision should be easy. The first thing you need to do is discover what it is that you have done in your life that has felt the most rewarding and that was aligned with your values and passions. This can help you discover what has been the most enjoyable and fun aspects of your life that also brought you a great reward. It is likely that your end vision will incorporate some of these activities.

The next thing you need to do is narrow down which of those activities were the most enjoyable and most rewarding. That way, you can discover what *specifically* you want to do. Then, you want to discover what your ideal outcome would be. In other words, what career would be the most enjoyable for you that would also create the results you desire in your life? Once you have, you can easily claim this as your end vision. All that is left to do is compare it against your values to make sure that it genuinely fits with your life and that it will be fulfilling in every aspect. Then, you can reverse-engineer it to get your near-future vision and to create the strategy for you to get there.

Building Your Core Brand Strategy

With your vision in mind, the next thing that you need to do is create your core brand strategy.

This is an actual action you are going to take to begin building the foundation of your brand and keep it strong and ready to be built upon to get you toward your end vision.

Your core brand strategy involves the key aspects of your brand: your image, your identity, and your outreach. Your image can be summarized as how you visually present yourself. In a personal brand, this should include yourself personally, your sense of style, a symbol or logo to represent you, and a color scheme that will represent you. You can also create a branding package for yourself that includes a color palette, your chosen fonts, your logo, and some sample images that show both the look and feel of how you want your brand to look. With this package, you can use it to determine how everything will be shared with your audience. Creating this image-based brand package will ensure that your look is consistent and identifiable and that people know what to expect with you. Your image will be at the core, as people are going to visually identify you based on what you show them.

Your identity is important as well. To secure your core strategy with your identity, you want to pay attention to keywords, catchphrases or mottos, your name, and your usernames and domain names across the internet. Before you begin branding yourself publicly, decide what you want people to look up when they are looking for you. Do you want them to search for your name directly, or do you have a name you want to be identified as? For example, you could brand yourself as "James Adams" or you could brand yourself as "The Soccer Dude." What you choose is entirely up to you. Just know that this name needs to stay with you the entire way. Once you have chosen it, secure your username across all social media platforms and as a domain name. This will ensure that as you grow out into your various outreach methods, your name remains consistent and therefore identifiable and easy to locate online. This means that your audience can easily follow you around. Purchasing and securing these beforehand is the best way to make sure that you do not begin branding yourself as one thing but later discover that the name is taken already on a different platform. That way, if you just want to start on one or two platforms before building out, you can.

The other aspect of your identity is who you are. The best way to secure this part of your core strategy is to write your ideal bio for yourself. However, write it as though you are someone else identifying yourself with another person. For example, "You should follow James Adams! He is a soccer announcer who is always sharing the latest soccer news, plus awesome jokes!" What you want to be known for needs to be considered in this way. That way, you can begin building yourself based on how you want others to identify you as well.

Lastly, your outreach is an important part of your core strategy. This is how you are going to actually get people to know who you are and what your image is. Your long-term outreach strategy should include the many different techniques and strategies outlined throughout this book. However, you may choose to design a starter strategy that is more manageable and effective for you. Attempting to master every single strategy at once can be overwhelming, thus making it a challenge for you to master any and potentially causing you to struggle to be seen at all. Instead, you want to identify how you want to begin your strategy and where you will go from there. Ideally, you should start on just one or two platforms online. Get the hang of these platforms and begin expanding your followers before moving to another platform to master those. This way, you can really get the hang of each one before moving on to the next. This type of strategy is more sustainable and will support you better in the long run.

Understanding What Goes Into Long-Term Strategy

With your immediate strategy in mind, you need to begin discovering what goes into creating your long-term strategy. This strategy is ultimately going to depend on what your vision is. Your long-term strategy does not need to be accounted for day-by-day, but it should include the key milestones that you want to pass and what it will take for you to pass them. For example, say your overall goal is to make $1,000,000 per year in business, but one year from today, you want to pass the $100,000 per year mark in your online sales business. You can easily use this as a milestone toward your larger goal, but a smaller goal to support you in creating your strategy to get there. That way, you can design a strategy to get from where you are now to this first milestone. Then, you can consider this first milestone to be the first part of your strategy in reaching your end-goal.

Creating multiple smaller milestones in this way not only identifies and outlines a strategy for you to get to your end-goal, but it also supports you in having a clear path for right now. Furthermore, these smaller goals mean that you can reassess your overall vision at each milestone and adjust your bigger strategy to make sure that you are truly aligned with this goal. While everyone would love for the drive from point A to point B to be extremely straightforward and clean cut, the reality is that many things will happen and change between now and then that will require you to adjust your strategy. Not becoming too attached to the long-term strategy and staying focused on what needs to be done to reach your next milestone on time is a great way to accommodate for these and to spend more time doing and achieving and less time planning and stalling. While a great vision is important, getting stuck on the vision and not taking any action will never help you achieve your goals.

Discovering What Motivates You

Lastly, a personal brand requires that you know how to motivate yourself. Simply put, you will not have the massive support in motivating yourself to move forward when it comes to personal branding that you might in other areas of your life where other people are concerned. Your personal brand is very personal to you and no one will care about it more than you do. If you are not able to motivate yourself to stay committed to your goals and keep moving forward, no one will be able to.

Knowing what motivates you and how you can keep yourself motivated is essential. Generally, we are motivated by our values and vision. However, there will be times that this simply does not feel like enough. Knowing how to create more instantaneous bursts of motivation, such as by setting shorter-term goals, rewarding yourself highly for reaching your goals, or celebrating yourself at each milestone can be a great way to keep yourself moving.

Another thing many people consider is their "why." Their why is essentially the reason why they are even doing what they are doing. Many people are motivated by their children, their families, their illnesses or disabilities, their living conditions, their desire for money or to travel, or otherwise. Knowing what exactly it is that you want and how your personal brand is going to get you there is a great way to keep yourself motivated in moving forward and building success.

As you identify what motivates you, be sure to write it down and keep it handy. Then, on those days that are particularly challenging and when you are unsure of what to do to keep yourself going, you can review the list and remember all of the ways that can keep you moving forward. That way, you will be sure to stay motivated, stay on track, and achieve your vision with your own support.

Chapter 4:
The Importance of Being You

When it comes to personal branding, a quote that is highly regarded is this: "Be yourself because everyone else is already taken" by Oscar Wilde. This quote reminds us that attempting to directly copy someone else's brand or trying to follow in our role models footsteps too closely can actually inhibit our success rather than support it. Just because someone else is successful at being them does not mean you will be. Likewise, no one will ever be as successful at being you as you will be.

Understanding the importance of being authentic in the business world is essential. This is especially true in personal branding. Look at it this way, if you were to build an entire brand around someone you are not, the charade would become exhausting. Although it may earn you success in the short-term, in the end, people are going to recognize that you are not being authentic. The feel behind your marketing will be completely off, your commitment and dedication to your brand will be minimal, and your emotion will be stand-offish. No matter how much you try to tell yourself or your audience that this is in fact who you are, you will find yourself feeling exhausted, overwhelmed, frustrated, and maybe even a little bit neurotic when trying to keep up with it all. The only way to avoid that is to make sure that you are being authentic when you brand yourself.

Another reason why branding yourself is important is that as you go on with your brand, you will get to know yourself on a deeper and deeper level. This means that any decisions you make with your personal brand will be deeply aligned with who you truly are, thus making them a great decision for both you and your brand. This level of authenticity will shine through and ensure that you experience tremendous success all around.

When it comes to personal branding, you want to be able to sit and look back on your life one day and realize that everything you did was authentic and true to you. One of the many reasons why people embark on personal branding is because they want to live a life that is more suited to *them*. How tragic would it be to realize that this was one of your driving factors, but to look back and realize that you rejected it entirely in favor of being who you thought you were supposed to be?

In being yourself, you allow yourself the gift of being true. You also give that gift to your audience. Furthermore, this will actually support you in standing out from the crowd and being more unique and easy to identify for your audience. This means that every quirk, flaw, difference, and "strange" thing about you is actually a powerful tool for you in marketing your personal brand. These are aspects of you that make you very real to your audience, which makes you even more enjoyable. People want to see, follow, and support others who are being real and who are authentically expressing themselves. The truth is, far too few of people are willing to actually do that, so seeing it will not only help you get your message out but will inspire your audience to feel more confident and comfortable within themselves.

Identifying who you are and using this as a way to brand yourself is important. This is not only about inspiring yourself and being an inspiration to others, but it is actually a key branding strategy when it comes to personal branding. To effectively brand yourself to your audience, there are a few strategies and practices that you can do to identify your unique self in a better way. Here is what they are:

Identify What Makes You Unique

The first step in this practice is to write out a list of everything that makes you different from the others. This includes any quirk, trait, flaw, passion, or piece of your personal history that is unique from others' experiences.

This list is going to help you discover what is different about you that virtually no one else can claim or identify with. Although you will obviously share overlapping traits with others, this particular list is entirely unique to you. Seeing it out on a list will help you recognize how different you are and what stands you apart from others. It will also help you determine which of these may actually support you in your personal branding. Be sure to include everything on this list, even the items that seem unimportant. You may later come to realize that they are actually very important elements to add into your unique *you*-based brand!

Prioritize This List

With your list completed, prioritize what items on the list you identify with the most. This will help you see what is most prominent in making you uniquely you and what is least. This can be prioritized based on what is the most different or unique, and what is the most common in your personality.

Blend Your Traits With Your Vision

Now, with your list completed and prioritized, you can blend it with your vision. To do this, determine what traits actually support you in reaching your vision. For example, if you want to be known for making the best bread in the world and you have a preference for keeping your kitchen *just so* or you favor one particular ingredient in your bread over anything else, this can be unique to you. Highlighting and amplifying this can make it much easier for you to discover what makes you different from anyone else and how this sets you apart from the rest of the crowd. It also supports you in knowing which of your unique aspects blends best with your vision, helping you to actually use these characteristics as marketable traits.

Identify Yourself

Now, you want to identify yourself once again. If you will recall, in chapter 3, you were encouraged to introduce yourself to someone else as though you were not actually yourself. So, pretend that you are your own follower and that you are telling a friend about your account. How would you identify yourself and how would this particular quirk or trait tie into that description? Are you the witty bread maker? The sarcastic shoe cobbler? The heroic horse whisperer? The soccer dad who loves making dad jokes? What is your identity?

Once you know how you want to be identified, you can easily begin building your personal brand around this persona. In this aspect, you want to remain true to who you are, but you are being more selective about which aspects of yourself you are going to amplify the most. The reason is that these particular aspects of yourself are the ones that are going to set you apart, thus making you more likely to be noticed and picked apart from others in the same space as you.

With this identification, you want to tie in all of your marketing around it. Any time you are writing content, sharing images, or otherwise interacting with your audience, look for a way to tie these particular traits in with your brand. There will likely be more than one as people are multifaceted and you do not want to come across as dense or boring, so take advantage of this and share all of the quirks, parts of your history, traits, and flaws that make you unique and overlap with your vision. This helps people get to know you more intimately, gives you a great angle to share from, and builds the relationships between you and your audience.

Chapter 5:
Defining Your Audience

As with any brand, knowing how to define your target audience is important. A great way to think of this when it comes to personal branding is, who do you want to network with the most? In other words, who do you get along with most and who are you most interested in spending time with online and offline?

Attempting to gain the interest and attention of everyone is only going to ensure that you are not successful in being seen or recognized in the online space. Your better objective is to pay attention to who you specifically want to be liked by and focus on building your brand around catering to them.

A great way to begin identifying who you actually want to spend time with and who your ideal audience is would be to imagine the following scenario and consider your answer:

You walk into a social gathering that has gathered around your favorite topic. Immediately, you notice three groups of people. Upon taking a moment to notice each group, you decide which one you feel the most attracted to and decide to walk up to them and begin engaging in a conversation with them. The question is: who are they, what attracted you to them, and what are you hoping to engage in with them?

By identifying the answer to the above scenario-based question, you get a solid idea of who you actually like and who interests you the most. Remember, your personal brand needs to be personal to you. Attempting to appeal to an audience that does not actually resonate with you will likely only result in you feeling like an outcast because you struggle to fit in effectively. Instead, you want to identify where you fit in. If where you currently fit in and where you want to fit in is different, this is a great opportunity to practice self-development so that you can begin fitting in with your desired audience. In that case, choose your desired audience or the one that you personally would like to be acquainted with the most and honor this personal growth in yourself.

Once you have a better idea of who you want to be in your audience, you need to actually define your target audience. This means that you need to get very specific on what the demographic, who is in the audience, and why you are both interested in engaging with each other. You also need to determine how you are going to approach them and create a relationship with them since they presently have no idea who you are and you are the one wanting to build the relationship.

There are three steps in creating your audience and then recognizing who they are. Remember that in business, who you want to be your audience and who they actually are can change. Even in personal branding. This means that as you go on with the strategies in this chapter, you might find that the people responding best to your content are completely different from who you anticipated. In this case, there are two things you can do: adjust your ideal target audience or adjust your strategy. If you are happy with the response you are getting, adjusting your ideal audience grants you the opportunity to carry on with the momentum you are already building. If you are feeling completely unhappy with the audience you are currently targeting, adjusting your strategy is a good way to help yourself appeal to the audience you prefer. That being said, make sure that any adjustments you make still align with your values and vision so that you do not stray away from who you truly are in favor of appealing to your ideal person.

Step One: Empathize With Your Audience

The first step in identifying your audience is empathizing with them. If you have an idea of who you are targeting, you can begin discussing topics and challenges that resonate with this ideal audience. Be crystal-clear in establishing empathy toward this audience, letting them know that you identify with what their problems are and you understand why they are such a challenge. This supports you in building relationships with your audience and begins to identify you as "one of them."

You can easily empathize with your audience through your social media platforms, as well as anywhere else that you are presently performing outreach such as on your blog, in email newsletters, in forums, or anywhere else.

In addition to showing your audience that you identify with them and that they can relate to you and vice versa, empathizing with your audience also begins discussions. By engaging in these discussions, you can determine exactly what it is that these people are identifying with, what their hopes and dreams are, what they are looking for, and how your personal brand might be able to better serve them. In this case, it is not only a great way to define your target audience, but also to begin creating a business that will serve them.

Step Two: Create Your Offer

The next step in building your personal brand, making sales, and defining your target audience is creating a customized offer for the audience you identified in step one. This customized offer should be based on everything you learned about your audience, supporting you in creating an offer that directly supports them in having their needs met. This means that they are more likely to be interested in your offer, thus helping you maximize your engagement and make sales right off the bat.

This offer is going to do three things for you: increase exposure, earn sales, and perform market research. Through this offer, you are going to have people purchasing from you as long as you have crafted it correctly based on your demographic. The most important aspect of all of this, however, is that you are going to see exactly who within your overall demographic is actually purchasing what you are creating for them. This particular demographic will be far more defined, making *them* the ones you want to cater to. For example, if you know that moms in their 20s and 30s are your primary demographic but that moms between the ages of 28-34 who have more than one kid are your biggest purchasing audience, then you know specifically who you want to cater your brand toward. This goes for any audience. The more defined audience will be drawn not from those who engage the most, but from those who are actually willing to purchase from you.

If you are not yet ready to make sales, you might consider making a free offer that allows people to join you in an online live event, download something you have made for them, or otherwise engage with you in a way that requires for them to actually commit to something. This particular will not earn you money nor will it give you an exact idea of who is willing to pay for your content versus who is simply willing to accept the free offer, but it will give you a stronger idea of the demographic you are targeting. This is a great idea if you are not yet ready to design an offer or if you are still trying to navigate the waters in which you are wading.

Step Three: Improve Exposure and Conversions

The analytics you draw in through your sales are going to tell you who you are targeting that are actually purchasing from you. Through this information, you can begin refining your outreach to increase your effectiveness at reaching your ideal target client and converting them into customers. This process of refining your outreach and monitoring your analytics is the best way to see who responds best to you and how you can get them to respond even better. Through this action, more information regarding your target client will begin appearing in your analytics and you can get even better at relating to them, identifying the problems that they are having, and creating solutions that you can sell them.

Creating Your Audience "Profile"

With the analytics rolling in from your previous offer and the conversions that you have made, you will want to begin creating your audience's profile. This will essentially be a specific profile of who is in your audience, what defines them, what their motivations are, any opportunities you have to serve them, and what you can do to serve them better. Knowing this person specifically and doing all that you can to understand them ensures that you know exactly who you are talking to and how you should be talking to them in order to help them resonate better with you.

The best way to do this is to create an identity profile that outlines one specific person in your audience. This person should be the ideal character that defines who you are talking to, thus making them the "mascot" of your audience. For that reason, they do not need to be a real person. Instead, they can be a profile you create based on the summary of all of the information that you are learning through the audience.

Your profile needs to contain the following information:

- Age
- Gender
- Career
- Hobbies
- Location

You should also include anything relevant to what you are doing. For example, if you are creating a family-based brand, you would want to include information about the age range of the family, whether the parents are together or not, how many children they have, and anything else relevant to what you are aiming to do.

The more you detail your description of your ideal audience and understand who they are and why this makes them ideal for your brand, the easier it will be for you to identify how you can share with them. Be specific and include anything that you think will be relevant.

Some people will even include a name and an ideal image of who their audience looks like, typically found in a stock image on Google. This can be helpful in supporting you in narrating a dialogue between yourself and your audience, but it is not necessary. If you do choose to do this, keep the image handy and any time you are going to share something with your audience, run it by your ideal profile. See how the information serves them, whether or not it supports you in generating success, and if you can do anything to have a more effective interaction.

Identify Your Opportunity to Serve

Now that you have identified your audience, you need to define their problems and look for opportunities to serve them. Looking at who they are and determining their likely needs based off of their profile are a great way to begin understanding what your audience needs and how you can fulfill that need. You can then go ahead and begin creating opportunities for yourself.

For example, say your audience is the elderly people who are struggling to get around their house. You identify that they are likely those who are mostly living on their own with success but that their mobility is an issue. Their need, then, is being able to move around on their own while feeling safe and steady. That way, they can continue to live on their own for much longer. Your opportunity would be to create a solution to serve their mobility needs, whether it be selling products that make their mobility safer or designing a service that allows a support aid to come to their house on a set schedule to support them in accomplishing the tasks that require more mobility than they can comfortably handle.

When you know who your audience is and what they need, you can create products or services that support them in having that best life. This will help guarantee your sales. The understanding of all of this information will support you in creating a strong brand that supports you in getting those sales, however.

Chapter 6:
Personal Branding on Facebook

Personal branding on social media is essential. Knowing how to brand effectively across each platform will ensure that you are able to reach your market with the greatest success. That way, you can guarantee the effectiveness of your efforts. As social media continues to evolve, the strategies that you will be required to use will adjust. The strategies within this chapter are going to support you in personal branding on Facebook in 2019. It is important that you pay attention to trends as they adjust and shift and that you take the time to understand and master new features as they are constantly introduced. This will ensure that you are staying ahead of the trends and that you remain relevant, thus keeping your brand relevant and supporting you in staying exposed and noticed by your target audience.

The Value of Facebook in 2019

In 2019, Facebook is still the leading social media site in terms of having a large, diverse audience that can be tapped into for virtually anyone. Starting as a social media platform to connect friends and family across the globe to minimize the feelings of separation through the support of the internet, many have continued to use this platform for just that. Only, nowadays people are also using it as a powerful online networking tool. Features like groups, group chats, and pages are allowing individuals to connect with those they have never met before in a way that allows them to become friends and stay connected through the internet.

The one thing you really need to continue paying attention in 2019 is that everything you do in any form of public setting can be held against you on social media. This means that if you do anything that could take away from the personal brand that you are attempting to build and someone photographs you and shares it online, it is there for everyone to see. This is particularly troubling on Facebook where tagging can happen and virtually everyone has a profile so they can see your tags. For that reason, you need to be very cautious about who you spend your time with, where, and what you are doing. If you build your personal brand to authentically represent you, as we discussed in chapter 4, then you can feel confident that your reputation online and offline should continue to uphold and this should not be an issue.

Aside from having to make sure that you behave in a way that protects your reputation, Facebook gives you a vast and diverse platform to begin building your reputation organically. You can easily create a personal profile that you use for outreach, as well as a page and a group. There are so many unique tools available to you that you can use to begin engaging with others. As long as you use it properly, you can rapidly build your network, make meaningful connections, and begin building reputations not only between you and your audience but your brand and your audience as well.

Building Your Reputation

Building your reputation online is everything. Your reputation is going to be entirely based off of all of the information that you identified earlier in this book. Everything that you need to support your vision, connect with your audience, and make your personal goals will be incorporated. This can be identified within the identity you defined for yourself in chapter 4.

As you build your reputation, it is essential that you understand that every single interaction, engagement, and action you take on Facebook is going to serve this greater reputation. You cannot do anything online that would compromise this reputation and prevent you from being able to fulfill your goals by taking away from how others see you. This may sound intimidating, but it truly is not. The goal here is to make sure that you act in a way that is authentic and genuine toward who you are, what you desire to achieve, and how you share yourself with the world around you. Then, you need to be clear and concise in how you are sharing this with others.

Creating a reputation online, particularly on Facebook, will be defined based on where you spend your time, who you make friends with, and how you communicate with them. When you understand these three elements, it becomes much easier to create a strong reputation on your Facebook page.

Where you spend your time includes what pages and groups you are engaging in the most. If you are engaging in groups and pages that align with your vision and support your goals, you can easily share and network with people who are supportive. If you are engaging in areas that contradict your goals, however, you will quickly find yourself sullying your reputation by directly contradicting who you are trying to brand yourself as.

The friends you keep on Facebook matter, too. For example, if you are trying to brand yourself as a friendly and positive person but you have pessimistic and negative people regularly commenting on everything you share, this reflects negatively on you. To prevent this from happening, refrain from adding anyone who is in direct contradiction with your brand. If you cannot do this (say you do not want to hurt a family member's feelings), you can always adjust your privacy settings on your posts to exclude that particular person from seeing what you are sharing.

How you communicate with people includes what you are saying, what language you are using, and how you are supporting them. You want to keep this positive, on-brand, and supportive. The more helpful and kind you communicate, while also maintaining the right vernacular for your demographic, the more approachable and likable you will be by your desired audience. This will support you in creating a strong reputation for yourself that supports others in wanting to connect with you further.

Populate Your Information

On your Facebook page, a key part of branding is to make sure that you populate your profile, page, and group with plenty of information. The digital age has made people somewhat nosy, and they always want to know more. If people come across you and like what they see, they are going to want to browse your profile, page, and group to learn more about you. You need to have something for them to learn about! Boring pages that do not feature any interesting information informing them of who you are will result in the individual leaving your account once again because there is nothing to attract them and draw them in. However, an account with the "About" section filled out and more information about who you are, as well as a page and group with descriptions and stories fully filled out, give interested individuals plenty to read about. This means that they can learn plenty about you before actually deciding whether or not they want to engage with you.

It may seem heinous to have someone want to read everything about you first and then get to know you second, but this is how things work on Facebook. People are generally cautious about who they spend their time with, even online, and who they are willing to share their more personal information with. Having a profile that is well-populated with plenty of consumable information can help these individuals feel confident in choosing to communicate with you. It also helps them know what to expect. Furthermore, if you are selling products or services online, they may even find themselves interested and ready to purchase without ever having to go through the long process of getting to know you first. So, not only is this a great way to encourage networking by showing your audience that you are open and friendly, it also gives them a chance to see what you are all about and choose to purchase if they so desire.

Create a Friendly Profile

A profile, page or group needs to be friendly and engaging if you want people to actually want to befriend you or follow you online. Doing so requires three things: pictures that look friendly and open, content that is engaging and helpful, and an invitation or reason to follow you.

Your picture on Facebook should be something that clearly captures who you are and highlights your most notable feature. A great headshot, an image of you doing something you love such as taking photographs or spending time with your family, or a full body image of you all make for great pictures that can be used in your profile. The key importance here is to choose an image that is clear and high-quality, one that is illuminated enough that they can easily see the features on your face, and one that makes it very clear which person you are in the image.

Your content needs to be something that supports your ideal audience in immediately feeling as though they need to befriend, follow, or join you in the online space. Creating contents that are relevant, relatable, engaging, helpful, informative, entertaining, or inspirational is a great way to do just that. People like reading content with a purpose, especially when that purpose serves them, specifically. Keeping your content directed at serving others is a great way to give your audience a strong reason to add you as a friend, follow your page, or join your group on Facebook.

Lastly, you need to make it obvious that you *want* engagement from others. Particularly with personal profiles that are being used for branding and networking, people may feel confused as to whether or not they can add you. Making it obvious by adding a statement in your profile's bio on your personal page is a great way to encourage them to engage with you. If you want someone to follow your business page, you can always include a statement at the bottom of your posts that says "follow for more great content!" With groups, you can include a statement in the public group description that says something like "Join us for _____" so that you can identify who best fits within the group and invite that specific person to join you. This will work as a call to action, letting people know that you want to be engaged with and giving them the encouragement to do the same with you.

Update Frequently

Posting regularly is an essential way to stay relevant and connected with your audience. Ideally, you should be posting to Facebook about 3 times per day. You should also be spending a few minutes each day commenting, liking, and engaging with other people. This will be considered your networking time! Keeping your audience updated on what you are doing, sharing purposeful content, and engaging with your audience is the best way to make sure that you are regularly getting your name in front of them. That way, they can begin to identify who you are, understand what you are all about, gain value from you, and stay close with you online.

If you are networking in multiple areas on Facebook such as in profiles, pages, and groups, you want to spend time updating each of these unique areas. So, three updates on each of these three areas would suffice. This may sound like a lot, but it does not actually take long. Furthermore, you can always write or create inspired content ahead of time and schedule it to post to your account, page, or group using a third-party application like Hootsuite or Buffer. This is a great way to stay up-to-date without having to personally schedule aside fixed time each day to get online and update people. Then, all you have to do is make sure that you hop online to engage with people on a daily basis.

Going into 2019, the best way to keep people updated is through video marketing. People absolutely love videos that share great content by educating or entertaining them. Product demonstration videos, live Q&A videos, sharing a short clip of the goings on of your day or something relating to your brand, or otherwise sharing video content that supports your brand and reputation is a great way to take advantage of videos. Ideally, you should focus on creating professional and well-put-together videos as well as live videos that are filmed in real-time.

Another great area to share on in Facebook right now is stories. Facebook stories allow you to share exclusive, behind-the-scenes images of your life and brand with your audience. This helps bring them into your world and feel a greater connection to you, thus supporting you in having an even greater relationship with your audience. One great tip to know is that if you link your Instagram and Facebook together, you can share Instagram stories to your Facebook feed. This means that both audiences can be nurtured by the same story-sharing activity.

Build Your Community

The last key strategy you need to pay attention to and nurture on Facebook in 2019 is your community. Groups are all the rage right now, and for good reason. When you run a group, it is your primary commitment to nurturing that group, share purposeful content that gives others a reason to stick around and facilitates the networking that goes on within the group. Building a community in this way gives people a great opportunity to get to know each other and yourself, and it puts you at the top of the community. This means that if everyone can only identify one single person in the group, it is pretty good that the one person they are identifying is *you*.

In your community, you gain the opportunity to network, build personal connections and relationships, and facilitate market research for your brand. You can easily see who makes up your demographic within your audience, how they interact, what their problems are, how you can fulfill them, and any opportunities that may arise for you to better serve your audience. This type of hands-on, in-the-thick-of-it-style marketing research is something that is extremely new to marketing. Being able to be this hands-on and involved in your community means that not only will you be seen as approachable and friendly, but that you can also tailor your entire brand to serve your audience.

If you do not presently have a group, identifying the opportunity to create one, designing a specific focus, and building your community is essential. This key marketing strategy will serve you in many major ways especially in 2019, so begin taking advantage of it right now if you want to make the most of it.

Chapter 7:
Personal Branding on Instagram

Personal branding on Instagram is growing to be just as popular as Facebook. Instagram does vary slightly from Facebook, however, as the demographic it targets is far more focused than those who spend time on Facebook. On Instagram, the common demographic is between the ages of 25-34 years old. This means that if your brands' demographic falls in this particular range, which most online brands' customers do, Instagram will be a powerful area for you to spend time. Spending time building your brand on Instagram is ingenious for personal brands, as this tool provides great outreach for individuals looking to grow a large following, create a strong ability for their audience to visually identify them, and share in a way that provides optimal organic reach tools.

The Value of Instagram in 2019

Getting on Instagram gives you a great opportunity to take advantage of creating a more personalized, visual brand in a sometimes cold and segregated community. For a long time, social media was known as being impersonal and disconnected because of the very nature that people were not getting together and networking in a powerful way. Adding in the visual element and taking advantage of the growing trend of creating genuine engagement between you and your audience is the main objective of Instagram especially in 2019, and Instagram provides you with all of the necessary tools to create this connection and develop this relationship.

Another reason why getting on Instagram is important to your brand is that many of Instagram's users actually use the platform to locate companies and influencers that are representing "the small guy." In other words, many are looking to get away from supporting faceless, soulless corporate structures and begin supporting individuals, small companies, and local businesses. By getting yourself on Instagram, you put yourself directly in front of an audience who is looking for exactly what and who you are. This means that not only do you have a demographic perfectly suited to your target, but you also have one that is eagerly ready to consume any content you are putting out for them.

Building Through Authenticity

The big key in social media in 2019, as you are now well aware of, is being authentic and sharing the real aspects of who you are. That being said, it is no surprise that Instagram is going to really be a strong tool for anyone who shows up and shares in an authentic manner. The fact of the matter is that there are hundreds of thousands of photographs out there that all look basically the same, just like the different models or people in them. While it is incredible to see everyone sharing, it has led to a desensitization of sorts in the world of Instagram. Many people find

78

themselves scrolling these images just for pure pleasure and rarely actually following the accounts or engaging with them. This is because there are simply too many and none stand out enough to really make them worth following over the others. Instead, if they like the aesthetics, they will simply follow the hashtag (a feature that was newly introduced in 2018.) To avoid getting ignored in favor of a hashtag, make sure that you let your authenticity actually shine through in your images. While high-quality images and high-resolution photography is a must, doing the same thing everyone else is doing should be avoided at all costs.

At one time, everything was done with the intention of having the most likes and follows, but this time is long gone. Most potential followers and eventual customers do not give any concern to the number of followers or likes a person accumulates on social media. Instead, they want to see that your content and the things you are sharing are genuine and authentic. They should stand out, be different, and highlight those unique aspects of yourself that we covered in chapter 4. If you can fill your feed with images that represent yourself in an authentic, genuine, and unique manner, you will have far more luck in getting real followers who are sincerely there to support you and pay attention to what you are sharing. This means that your account will see far higher engagement and more conversions out of your followers turning into paying customers.

Creating a Strong Instagram Strategy

On Instagram, the strategy is extremely necessary. Because of the nature of how "busy" the application is with so many users frequently uploading pictures and sharing them with the same hashtags that you are, you need to make sure that you are following specific practices to boost your profile and get greater exposure and engagement. The strategy you need will feature three steps: an attractive feed, consistency in posting, and regular genuine engagement.

Having an attractive feed will support you in being followed because, true to the nature of visual marketing, your audience cares about your aesthetic. This does not necessarily mean they are looking for a generic magazine-style feed. Instead, it means that they want something coherent, that looks good together as a whole, and that looks like you genuinely put thought into your posts. Downloading an app like PLANN which can support you in uploading images to your Instagram and dragging them into order to make them more aesthetically appealing is a great way to make your page more attractive. This makes it more interesting and engaging for the human eye, thus increasing your likelihood of individuals tapping "follow." The key here is making sure that you use the same filters, color schemes, and general lighting in your images. If you upload quotes, make sure they are based on a similar template that looks attractive as well.

Consistency is your next key. The general consensus is that posting three times per day will keep your feed active, at the top of peoples' pages, and easy to locate for new followers. This is a great rule of thumb, however, it is not entirely necessary. You may find that it is a challenge to discover and curate enough high-quality images to build a feed that rapidly. Depending on what you are posting, you can always draw stock images from websites like Unsplash or Pixabay, though this may take away from your authentic angle if you post too many. So, if you are choosing to tone it down in favor of having higher quality authentic content, you can lower your posting to just one or two times per day. The biggest key element here is posting on a daily basis. That being said, you do not want to go above three times per day as this can have you seen as spammy and can actually reduce your visibility and increase the number of unfollows you get.

Lastly, you need to engage. Engaging with your audience on a regular basis shows that you are there to network and encourages them to network back with you. Like the pictures of those that you follow, comment as often as you can, and always comment back when people comment on your posts. Commenting is virtually always the best way to go on Instagram in terms of building engagement. This is because likes are dished out so frequently that most people scroll over those notifications or ignore them in favor of the more "rare" notifications: comments and follows. As you comment, make sure that you are being authentic. Write each comment out at the moment, even if it seems like a hassle. Doing this shows that you are genuinely engaged. It also refrains from being ignored or marked as spam for sprinkling copy-and-paste comments all over Instagram.

Taking Advantage of Stories and IGTV

Instagram has spread out into stories and IGTV as newer ways to share with your audience and help bring them into the behind-the-scenes of your life. These two unique sharing aspects allow you to engage with your audience in new ways, making it even easier for you to share and encourage followers to join you, watch you, and remember who you are.

Instagram stories are images or videos that you share that are only viewed for a few seconds and then completely disappear after 24 hours. However, Instagram also introduced something called "Story Archives" which appear on your profile. These archives are stories that you have saved and organized onto your profile in specific categories. Many brands are using them to share the key elements of their brands with other people. For example, if you are a fashion brand, you might have a "Fall 2019" category for archived stories. Then, any Fall fashion you spot can be snapped, added to your stories, and saved in a compiled list within the archive. This means that followers can see these archived stories whenever they want until you intentionally delete them.

Stories also offer two great marketing strategies that will help you dominate marketing in 2019. The first one is suspense marketing. Sharing images with your audience that gives a small insight as to what you are doing or what you are about to release without giving the full details or full demonstration is a great way to get people seeing what you are doing and have them start asking questions. The buildup of anticipation makes them far more interested and more likely to click to learn more when you finally launch or share whatever it is that you are actively in the process of launching.

Another way of marketing in your stories is through links. If you have 10,000+ followers, Instagram introduces a link-sharing feature that allows you to include clickable links in your stories. Viewers simply swipe up on the story and can see a link (or any links) that take them to whatever it is that they desire to see. This is a great way to market different things shown in your story or to market one specific thing in general. It is done by simply tapping the chain link icon that appears in the top right corner of your screen after reaching 10,000 followers on Instagram.

Instagram TV, or IGTV as the app calls it, is a video sharing feature that allows users to share videos up to an hour long that are stored on their channel. This channel can be comprised by any creator or Instagram user that chooses to upload content, allowing them to share anything they desire with their audience. Marketers and personal brands are using this to educate their audience, share new products through demonstrations, do "get ready with me" style videos, perform Q&A videos, and otherwise market through video sharing. This new tool has brought an entirely new layer of marketing to Instagram that has allowed personal brands to share far more, making it even easier to interact with and engage with your audience on Instagram while also providing valuable content that earns you greater followers. Anyone who follows you on Instagram can see your channel. You can upload to your channel directly through the Instagram app on your phone by tapping the IGTV icon on the top right corner of the main feed.

Optimizing Your Page's Branding

As with all profiles, you are going to want to optimize your Instagram account for your branding. When someone lands on your account, they should quickly be able to determine who you are, what you are doing, and what they can learn or gain from your account. This means that you need to have a username that reflects your brand, your name clearly displayed at the top of your page, a bio that explains what you do and what your personal mission is, any relevant link to find you elsewhere, and a feed that shows a visual of what you are sharing with other people on a regular basis.

Your name on Instagram is different from your username. Whereas your username is the name that people will use to find you, your name is what is displayed in bold font above your bio. Both the username and Instagram name need to be clearly displayed, easy to understand, and well-represented. Here is where having the same username across all social media platforms and your domain name already purchased is going to serve you. The username that you use should be what your brand is. If you yourself are your own brand, it should be your personal name. If your name is hard to spell, however, you might adjust it slightly and make that your brand. For example, Gary Vaynerchuk is a challenging name to spell so the famous influencer uses Gary Vee as his online persona to make him easier to recognize and find in the online space. If you have a brand name you are going by, or a title you identify with, you might use that instead. For example, "The Celestial Psychic" (@thecelestialpsychic) or "The Salad Spoon" (@thesaladspoon). Keep your username easy to spell and easy to identify. This will make it easy for people to find you and to remember you so that they can find you again. Your name, however, should simply be your first and last name. Again, that is unless your name is particularly challenging to spell, pronounce, or remember, then you may choose to swap it out in favor of an initial or a middle name.

The next thing you need to optimize is your profile image. This image should not be larger than what you see on your profile, so ideally it needs to be something that is easy to see in the small image. The best images for these profile shots are either headshots, a picture of your logo, or an image that captures what you share on your page and represents your "theme." Keep them clear and high resolution with a very clear focus, as this will ensure that your potential viewers are not confused by what they are seeing and overlooking your account thinking that you are just another user and not someone worthy of being seen.

Creating the Ability to Get Seen

Lastly, you need to master the art of getting seen on Instagram, namely, hashtagging. Using hashtags on Instagram is the way that people are discovered. Instagram allows for each individual to tag up to 30 hashtags in their image, allowing you to use up to 30 popular tags that can expose you to tens of thousands, hundreds of thousands, or even millions of potential viewers. Using these tags properly can get you seen by a massive audience and can support you in getting far more follows and significantly more engagement.

There are two particular "rules" you need to follow when it comes to using hashtags on Instagram. The first rule is that you should never share the hashtags in the caption of your image *unless* it is a single extremely relevant one, or a custom one that you are using to help your audience engage with you. In this case, one or two is fine. However, the bulk of your hashtags should actually be placed within the first comment of your image within 30-45 seconds after posting your image. This ensures that your image gets engagement quickly, which supports Instagram's algorithm in pushing you up further in the feed so that you can get seen by a larger audience. That being said, you should pre-write your hashtag group out in a note on your phone then copy it so that as soon as you hit "share" on your image, you can instantly jump into the comments section and post your hashtags.

The second rule is that you never want to use hashtags that are barely seen, nor do you want to use hashtags that are overused. There are some exemptions here, however. For example, if you are working on using a particular hashtag to engage with your audience, then you have likely decided to use one that has never been used before. Creating your own in this way naturally means that no one else has used it, thus it is not seen often. This would be a fine usage of one that is rarely used. You can also use ones that are rarely used if they are very specific toward your audience. In this case, the few that do see the hashtags are far more likely to engage, making it worth it. When it comes to using overused hashtags, you want to avoid this as much as possible. Using 2-3 per post is okay, but any more than that and you are wasting your time. Hashtags that are overused are used many times per day, meaning you will quickly get buried and the window of opportunity is significantly smaller for you. Instead, you want to have your window of opportunity enlarged by using hashtags that have more than 75,000 posts per tag and less than 999,999. This ensures that it is used often enough that you will actually get seen, but not so often that you will get buried. Again, use up to 30 but at least 15 hashtags. This will ensure that you gain maximum exposure.

When picking which hashtags to use, you can easily type in a popular hashtag and begin exploring the "see also:" hashtags are displayed whenever you choose a hashtag to view. This supports you in finding similar content that your audience is also viewing, which will make it easier for you to find your audience and use hashtags that they are using. That way, you are getting seen by the right demographic and you are using trending hashtags. Be sure to revisit these hashtags regularly as they will let you know what new trends are arising and what new hashtags to watch for. This will keep you relevant and trending as well, making it more likely for you to be seen. Be wary of hashtags that are not growing every few months or that do not have any recent shares, which can be determined by looking at the first 3-5 pictures shared in the "Most Recent" feed associated with that hashtag. These ones are likely dying trends that will result in you wasting a hashtag and not getting seen as easily by a relevant audience.

Chapter 8:
Personal Branding on Twitter

Twitter is another great platform for personal branding. This social sharing platform is one of the largest ones in existence, competing alongside Facebook, Instagram, and YouTube as one of the top social media platforms. Twitter has a vast demographic, making it a highly effective tool when it comes to marketing and branding. That being said, Twitter also has a very specific learning curve that people need to endure in order to get the most out of it. In this chapter, you are going to learn about why it is important for you to master this learning curve, what you can expect to get from it, and how you can master it.

The Value of Twitter in 2019

With over 1 billion users on Twitter, this platform is great for promoting your business, engaging in customer service, building relationships with influencers, and engaging with your ideal audience. Twitter is a platform that is based largely on having conversations with other people. The collective conversation is ongoing, supporting hundreds of thousands of people joining in on the conversation and sharing their opinion and engaging with others. When used properly, this will be your goal as well: to network and join in on the conversation. If you are lucky enough, you may even become a topic of one of the positive conversations, getting your name even further out there by making you go viral.

Twitter is a great platform to see what is trending and to stay relevant. It revolves largely around what people are talking about right now which makes this platform great for getting involved but also phenomenal for tracking your demographic and seeing exactly what they are interested in, what they are talking about, and what is relevant to them right now. This means that you can both get involved and follow the trends of what your active audience is interested in so that you can curate content specifically based on what they are actively talking about and paying attention to. As a brand, staying relevant and having trending content is one of the biggest things you need to stay on top of. If you begin talking about trends long after the fact or miss them altogether, those who are staying active and on top of things will definitely take over your audience and captivate their attention.

As well, because of the way Twitter is created, it is a great platform to use for customer service and support. If your personal brand performs sales of any form, users can easily jump onto Twitter and send you a direct message with regards to their question or concern. You can then easily address their question or concern and support them in finding the answer or solution they need. This is far easier than having to manage a company phone number or email, making your customer service both effective and modern.

Branding Your Twitter Account

Keeping your Twitter account well-branded is essential. 47.8% of people who land on your account are going to click over to visit your link, so long as they know what it is that they are looking at. So, having your account well-branded means that they know who you are and what you are offering, and they can then determine whether or not it is worth their while to go to that link and pursue anything you are selling them.

There are five ways to brand an account on Twitter including your cover image, your profile image, your bio, your custom link, and your pinned post. Each of these features should be properly branded in a way that compliments one another so that they can support your audience in understanding who you are in the greater picture and learning more about you.

For your profile image, you should keep it clean and simple. Most personal brands will use a clear head shot that has great lighting and shows off who they are. Alternatively, you can use an image of your logo. For Twitter, refrain from using anything generic or that looks like a stock image. Most people will skip over these types of images because they look like everyone else in the bunch. Your profile picture is going to appear next to everything you comment, share, Tweet, and Retweet so it really needs to be something that makes you stand out against the rest of the crowd but that continues to look professional.

Your cover image can easily be used to brand your business as well as to market anything you have going on. To do both, create a custom cover image using an app like Canva, complete with your brand colors and logo. Then, you can include a small image or caption about anything you are presently offering or selling, or even your motto or catchphrase. Branding your cover photo in this way will make it coherent with your overall image but will also use it as a way to share whatever your latest launch, milestone, or achievement is which will add texture to your account.

Your bio is where you get to share a bit about who you are in 160 characters or less. To brand this aspect, you want to share what you do with your potential follower in a way that clearly expresses your personality and highlights what is so unique about you in particular. Put it this way: there are probably already thousands upon thousands of people out there doing what you are doing. If you want to get seen over others, you need to share it from your unique voice, since the exact nature of your work may not be entirely unique to you. For example, there may be millions of virtual assistants out there, but you are the only one who brings your unique personality and traits to the virtual assistant scene. Maybe you are quirky, maybe you are highly knowledgeable about what your clients need and can do many things, or maybe you even like to train and educate other people on how to become virtual assistants. Use this angle and make sure you express it in your bio.

Your link allows your visitor to find you elsewhere on the net. You should use a link to your website that lets your visitor do the exploration on their own. This will guide them to the next step, and then they can choose what exactly it is that they are interested in learning about. Your website can provide them with the means to learn just that.

The last thing you need to brand is your pinned post. Twitter allows users to pin a Tweet, meaning that as a personal brand, you can pin any Tweet that supports you in marketing yourself and your brand to your visitors. This Tweet should change from time to time to prevent your page from looking stale. Most companies, brands, and influencers will actually change out their pinned Tweet and cover image simultaneously based on whatever they are actively marketing at any given time. This gives you a way to visually share an image of what you are marketing as well as provide more information on it through your pinned Tweet. Users that are interested can then go to your link and learn more about the offer. If you are talking about a specific offer being available at the "link in the bio," then you should adjust your URL to take them directly to that offer, rather than simply landing on your homepage.

Joining the Conversation and Networking

Twitter, as you know, is all about conversations. If you want to get involved with Twitter and begin building an engaged following, you need to be actively getting involved in these conversations. Doing so is not nearly as challenging as it may seem, even though there are literally hundreds of thousands of people, if not millions, participating in these collective conversations.

The best way to get involved is to discover the conversations through two strategies: the first one is to pay attention to "Trending Topics" on the browse page on your Twitter app. This page will show you what trends are taking over Twitter as a whole, allowing you to get in on conversations that are more generalized. When getting involved in these greater trends, make sure to stick to ones that directly reflect upon or resemble what your brand talks about. Choose things that your demographic is most likely to be interested in or that aligns with what you generally talk about online. Start by going to the trending hashtag and browsing what others are already saying. Then, begin engaging!

The next way is to follow people and influencers in your demographic or who cater to your demographic and see what they are talking about. They, like you, want to stay up to date on the latest trends. Following what they are saying can support you in getting ahead of trends and staying active on trends that are relevant to your particular niche. Again, simply follow a hashtag and begin getting involved in the conversation.

Whenever you feel like talking on a particular trending topic, make sure that you take advantage of hashtags and mentions. Hashtagging the topic or the trending hashtag relating to the topic will ensure that your Tweet gets seen. Tagging relevant people, influencers, or famous stars will support you as well in getting seen by their audience. This is also a great way to potentially get into a discussion with someone who has a massive following which can support you in having far more people engaging with you. On Twitter, this is a great way to increase your chances of going viral.

Self-Promoting Effectively

People who use Twitter as an exclusive means of self-promotion are not going to see much success with the app. Twitter is about networking, which means back and forth conversation. If you are talking about yourself excessively or trying to take all of the attention and put it on yourself, people are going to see this as fake and needy and they will likely overlook you. Twitter is not meant to be used as a way to make your feed look like a magazine or catalog or to bombard your followers with excessive self-promotion.

Naturally, however, you are going to want to self-promote your offers from time to time. This is the entire point of branding and marketing! However, there are specific ways to do it that will earn you great points in the online world, particularly with Twitter. The key times that you can market are when: you have something extremely exciting to share, or you are engaged in a conversation where you can offer a solution to the people you are sharing with.

When it comes to sharing exciting things, keep these self-promotions minimum and highlight only the truly exciting stuff. Ideally, these self-promotions should only make up about 20% of what you share on a weekly basis. They should also be shared in a way that is more of a soft share than a hard sell. For example, "My latest blog shares the best Spring 2019 decor! Check it out!" This type of post is engaging, interesting, and shows your audience what *they* are getting from reading your blog. "Read my post on Spring 2019 decor" however is a boring post and it sounds more about you than your reader. You need to keep things captivating, engaging, interesting, and mutually beneficial.

Sharing when you are in conversation should never be done in a pushy or spammy way. In other words, do not simply drop a link just because someone is describing a problem or situation that your product or service could fill the need of. Instead, engage in conversation with that person first and ask if you can share a solution with them. Asking for their permission first not only prevents you from looking like a fake account dropping spam and thus getting ignored, but it also makes it seem like it was the other person's idea for you to share it. This means that they are actually actively interested in what you are sharing and they are far more likely to actually follow up with you on the service or product you are offering. This will greatly increase your chances of making a sale. This is also a far more positive strategy for representing your brand, showing that you value relationships and genuine connections over hard sales, which will reflect positively on anyone who happens upon the thread and sees the engagement that took place between you and another individual. This means that you will also have a piece of permanent marketing out there for others to find as well.

Creating a Strong Twitter Strategy

Your strategy on Twitter is ultimately what is going to give you a clear focus on what you need to be doing and how much time you need to spend doing it. Not having a clear strategy can result in you becoming flaky and not remaining consistent, or it can result in you becoming obsessive and overusing the application and wasting valuable time that could be spent doing other things in your life. Having a strategy keeps you focused, on-track, and consistent with your account.

The best strategy for Twitter includes posting three or four times per day and spending approximately 30 minutes engaging with your audience and reviewing trending topics each day. This allows you to share organic content that you personally shared. It also allows you to engage with others and begin building strong connections, as well as earn the opportunity to share more about who you are and what you do. Lastly, spending this time on Twitter will help you conduct important market research so that you know what your audience is up to and what they are actively interested in. This means that you can gear your marketing toward these topics, offer new products and services that fulfill these needs or market gaps, and otherwise find ways to better serve and interact with your audience.

When posting on Twitter, it is important that you refrain from posting everything all at once. Scattering it out throughout the day will ensure that you gain consistent exposure over the day, rather than throwing everything out at once and minimizing your window of opportunity. If you do not have the time to go on Twitter several times per day to post at the moment, you can always use an app like Buffer to schedule posts that will automatically upload so that all you have to do is hop on and engage when you have time throughout the day. This can be a great way to maintain consistency, get your content out there, and minimize the amount of time you spend on social media on a day to day basis.

Chapter 9:
Personal Branding on
YouTube

YouTube is one of the oldest social media platforms around, and it has a strong ability to support people in marketing. In fact, it may be one of the most diverse and relevant marketing platforms for 2019. See, YouTube allows you to take advantage of video marketing which is highly trending right now. It also allows you to seamlessly integrate your videos into virtually anywhere. You can embed videos on your blog, share them on other social media platforms, embed them in emails, or simply promote them on YouTube to increase brand awareness. The versatility of the platform makes it an extremely valuable tool, especially in 2019 when video marketing is a massively growing trend. In this chapter, we are going to discuss how you can use YouTube as an independent platform, as well as how you can integrate it with other platforms to create more content for you to share across your other platforms.

The Value of YouTube in 2019

2019 will inevitably be the year of video marketing, making YouTube extremely relevant in the coming year. Beyond catering to the marketing strategy of choice for 2019, however, YouTube offers many incredible values to your business, with the biggest one being that the entire platform is built around creating a channel filled with videos. In the modern world, this is akin to having your own television network on cable TV.

Having a YouTube channel that is populated with informative, educational, interesting, or entertaining videos is a great way to create content for your audience to consume. This particular content gives you the unique opportunity to represent your personality, voice, and brand in a way that static images and status updates do not offer. You can also organize your channel effectively to create an entire viewing experience for your audience. If done right, as your page accumulates more videos for people to watch, you will likely find interested audience members binge-watching your content simply because they like your personality and what you are sharing. This is about the most personalized and customized your sharing can get, making your YouTube channel a highly valuable tool for your business.

Statistically speaking, YouTube has more than 1.5 billion active monthly users that collectively watch more than 5 billion videos per day. This is a massive audience to be catering to! If you upload your videos on a regular basis, cater directly to your demographic, and use your account properly, YouTube can be a major native and integrated marketing tool for you to use. Ultimately, getting on YouTube in one way or another is a no-brainer for anyone looking to brand themselves or their businesses.

One last benefit of YouTube is that your channel can earn you greater exposure, and it can also earn you a greater income. Having a Google AdWords account allows you to monetize your videos, meaning that YouTube pays you for these advertisements. While the income you can earn from this is not extremely large, it is enough that it adds a nice passive income stream as you expand your page and increase your exposure. This makes YouTube both a direct source of passive income, and a marketing tool to increase income within your own business.

Brand and Organize Your Profile

The first and foremost thing you need to do with your YouTube account is brand it. Branded accounts are far more likely to be easily identified by potential subscribers. Furthermore, an attractive branded account encourages people to stay around and browse. On the other hand, a messy one or a seemingly incognito one can result in people growing bored and moving on to the next account that is more aesthetically appealing.

To brand your profile, you will need to pay attention to and adjust six things. These include your profile picture, your channel art, your channel description, your 'about me' page, your introduction video, and the thumbnails that you use for your account. When these are branded, your account both looks great and it caters to your audience in a powerful way.

Your profile picture should once again be either your logo or a clean headshot of you. This makes it easy to identify and is really simple. If you choose a headshot, make sure you use great lighting and a clean background that is free of any distractions or harsh colors.

Your channel art can be customized and made on any application like Canva. This allows you to customize your own art to incorporate your brand, logo, and imagery. You need to make sure that any notable features are maintained within the center of your cover art, as your image will be cut down on mobile. It is essential that you optimize this for mobile as this will keep your page looking clean and professional. More than 500-million videos are viewed on mobile every day, so catering to this part of your audience is necessary.

Next, you need to update your description and about page. Your description is a short one or two sentence bio that will be featured directly on the main page of your profile. Your about page is a lot larger and can accommodate for more information. There, you can share information about who you are, what you are sharing, and why you are the best person to follow for the information or content that you are sharing on your channel. You can also include a point of contact so that if anyone wants to get in touch with you, they know how.

Lastly, you want to brand your thumbnails on your videos. Having a template you use on every single video will make it easier for people to identify your videos when they are browsing. Make sure you use the same template on every single video and that any images you upload into the template are high-quality and descriptive. This will ensure that your videos are both easy to identify and attractive to encourage more views.

Make Sure You Stick to Your Niche

One big mistake some personal brands will make on YouTube is venturing away from their niche to produce content. The idea of making a fun video that is outside of your niche and it potentially going viral is great, but doing so can actually distract from the purpose of your page. It also takes away from your professionalism. Make sure that all of your videos are on-brand, catering to your demographic, and focused on your niche.

If you want to change things up ever so often to add more diversity to your channel, consider instead making different styles of video that you upload. For example, maybe you have two minutes of "bite-sized" videos that offer quick inspiration, information, or entertainment for your audience. You can also have longer 10-15 minute videos where you share more, go into greater depth on bigger topics, or simply pack more entertainment into the video. When you create these different styles of video, pay attention to how your audience responds. The styles they respond best to should be emulated, maybe even turning into a standard style that you incorporate into your weekly strategy.

When you are playing with new styles, it is important that you still stay on topic and that each video continues to be packed with great information. Undermining the quality of your video by over-explaining unimportant topics, being vague or repetitive, or otherwise not packing in great value will result in people not watching as long. Too many videos like this can damage the quality of your overall channel and take away from your reputation. As a result, you may find yourself being unfollowed or struggling to gain followers in the first place. Keep your videos packed with juicy content that genuinely serves your audience and make sure that every video is full of high-quality information or entertainment.

Create a Strong YouTube Strategy

As with any platform, you are going to need a strong YouTube strategy. Most YouTubers create a strategy that revolves around comparing their channel to a cable TV station. If you were in love with a certain show, you would know that each week, it would air at the same time on the same days. So it should be the same with YouTube. Very few users will actually upload content every single day as this is typically a lot of work. Each upload requires you to film the video, edit it, and upload it to YouTube. At first, this may seem interesting and exciting. However, it can quickly become overwhelming as well. For that reason, you should always commit to a modest schedule early on. Maintaining just one or two videos per week is a great place to start. You can then increase this amount if you so desire, though it is not required.

In addition to determining how frequently you want to post, you should also consider what you want to post. This goes for content within the videos themselves, and if you want to do weekly or monthly themes for your videos.

When it comes to the videos themselves, you may want to start out with a single objective of what you want your channel to be known for. For example, if you are a baker, maybe you want your channel to be known for the best dessert recipes you can make in under 30 minutes. If you are an artist, maybe you want your channel to be known for showing people how to do different art techniques. If you are a professional marketing agent, maybe you want to share videos that are less than 5 minutes that educate people on how to market themselves better, or on current trends and how they can get on board with them and make the most out of them in their businesses and branding efforts. Having an objective and focus will help you determine what content to create, but it will also help your audience know what to expect.

If you want to have a strategy of how your videos are released, this can be helpful, too. For example, maybe every Tuesday you upload a short video that is a part of one segment you do, and every Friday you upload a longer video that is a part of a separate segment. Creating these segments and determining which days they will be released on helps your audience know what to expect, and it helps you know what to create and when. You can also create weekly or even monthly themes. For example, maybe on the first Wednesday of the month you always share product demonstrations that represent the products on sale that month. Or, the month before Christmas, you are going to do holiday-themed videos. Playing around with themes is another great way to add personality to your video and help people relate to your channel even further.

Consider Having a Personalized Intro

Many serious YouTubers have created personalized introduction clips that they feature at the beginning of each video. This is another great branding strategy that they use, even though it is not immediately visible on the page itself. However, whenever people see the intro or hear the music in it, they will recall you and your videos.

Intro videos are not too hard to create. There are many different styles that you can make, or you can outsource the creation to someone else. You can easily do this by sending them some of your best general footage of you in action and give them an idea of what you want it to be like.

The intro should be free of any copyrighted music, as this will inhibit your videos from being able to be uploaded. It can also lead to massive lawsuits and other problems from copyright infringement. Therefore, if you choose to create your own, make sure that you either purchase the rights to use the music, or you pick royalty free music.

Your intro should ideally introduce who you are, represent your brand well, and give your viewers an idea of where else they can find you online. You can also ask for them to subscribe to your channel by placing a "Subscribe" icon on the last image or footage shown right before the intro ends.

For YouTube, you want to aim to have your intro last only 15-25 seconds. Anything too long will be annoying for your viewers, making them less likely to binge watch your channel because they have to repeatedly jump past the intro. Anything shorter may not be long enough to offer enough information or even make the intro worth it. Keeping it short but informative gives you a form of consistency in every single video.

The only time you should refrain from using your intro video if you have one is if you are sharing single short clips that you are using for attention or to hopefully go viral. In this case, using your intro would take away from the clip and diminish your chances of getting attention. Also, you could easily include a short outro clip or image that brands your account and shows interested viewers or potential followers where to go to find you online.

Market Yourself as The Expert

The key benefit of YouTube, especially in professions that revolve around information and knowledge, is having the capacity to brand yourself as the expert. When you create your videos, the more knowledge, and the information you have to share in a way that allows you to speak with authority and certainty, the better.

This information allows you to educate others who are interested in learning more in a way that makes it clear that you know what you are talking about and that they can trust you. Creating informative, educational videos or even tutorials is a great way to share with your audience and show them that you are the trusted go-to source for all things in your niche.

Marketing yourself as the expert will go beyond simply posting great, informative, or educational content, however. You will need to be consistent. Being marketed as the expert on YouTube will come from three places: high-quality information that proves you know what you are talking about, a consistency that proves you have plenty to educate on, and an established presence elsewhere that proves you have a social hold. These three things will support you in being marketed as the expert.

Naturally, early on, you are not going to have the massive amount of content or the massive online following. Do not let this discourage you, however. Stay consistent in creating high-quality and informative content and continue sharing elsewhere online to build your reputation as well. The more you share, the better. This will continue to build your reputation over time and will help you accumulate more videos that show that you have plenty to share and talk about. This will then snowball and result in you getting seen by many others interested in what you have to talk about. Then, your brand and reputation will grow.

The general consensus is that you should always behave like you are playing in the big leagues even if you are just starting out. Create content and execute a strategy that is aligned with someone who is already promoting to thousands or even millions of followers. This will encourage you to think big, stay highly professional, and promote yourself on a level that actually ends up gaining you that level of traction.

Integrate YouTube With Other Platforms

Lastly, one of the best benefits of YouTube is the ability to integrate it with other platforms. Knowing how to integrate YouTube effectively will support you in maximizing your exposure on this platform, as well as give you great content to populate your other platforms with. The best key ways to share your YouTube channel and videos include link sharing, embedding, and sharing on other social media platforms.

When it comes to link sharing, there are many areas that you can share your videos. You can go to platforms like Instagram and update your link with your latest video, you can place the link on your blog, or you can engage in online forums and conversations and share your link in appropriate areas. You can typically also locate other unique or creative areas to share your link online. This is a great way to drive traffic to your page.

You can also embed the video. Embedding it on your website, in a blog post, or in the body of an email, if you have an email newsletter, is a great way to get your video out there. These videos can be seen right in the area where it is embedded, meaning viewers will not even need to navigate to a separate app or page to view the video. These types of videos can be shared independently or with commentary added to fill the body of the email, blog post, or page further.

Lastly, sharing with other social media sites should be a given. Each time you upload a video to YouTube, you should immediately share it to Instagram, Facebook, and Twitter, and give your viewers a strong explanation as to how your video is going to change their life or at least their day.

Chapter 10:
Mentors and Personal Role Models

Mentors and role models are powerful teachers and influencers that can support you in understanding how to better brand yourself, as well as motivate you to continue moving forward. Virtually, anyone with any amount of success in today's world will attest to the power of having mentors and role models to help you move forward. They support your growth in a powerful way that can only be understood once you actually have one. If you truly want to generate a great deal of success in your personal brand, hiring or locating a mentor and finding personal role models are important. However, it is also important that you do not just go to anyone. Finding the right fit is important. In this chapter, we are going to discover how you can find mentors and personal role models, how to qualify them, and how you can approach mentors specifically to get them to work with you.

Why You Need a Mentor

A mentor in the professional world is a no-brainer. It is also not a new concept. For many years, those who were just starting out in the industry or who were in the process of building a name for themselves were often mentored by influential individuals in their industry that would support them in understanding how to master the industry. Mentorship was a great honor bestowed upon people by the greatest in the industry. Being mentored is still a mark of excellence and necessity for anyone who wants to grow and become highly successful. Acquiring mentors is quite a bit different in this day and age, however, as most mentors are also working with a global audience just as you are.

Having a mentor is not just a benefit or a frivolous option, it is a requirement. Mentors give you the time and attention required to flourish. They listen to you, understand your problems and concerns, and support you in discovering solutions. They educate you on what it takes to become the best in your industry. They have been where you are and they know exactly how you can proceed to reach a great level of success. Furthermore, mentors will hold you accountable and keep you focused on achieving your goals. With a mentor, you have someone who recognizes your passion and devotion but also understands what it is like to have fears and doubts. Because they have been where you are, they know exactly what is required to talk you down from ledges, bring you back from doubt and fear, and inspire and encourage you to remember why you began in the first place.

A mentor will not only be a great ally in your professional success, but they will also be a great aid in teaching you the ropes. If you want to emulate the success of the greats, having someone who is a great mentor to you is mandatory. They will push you, give you some new perspective, and help you discover the answers to your questions and concerns. There is truly an endless number of reasons as to why you need to have a mentor in your life. Having one, especially if you want to have personal success in your personal brand, needs to be a high priority for you. As you begin to grow and get serious about your success, having a mentor is high up on your list of things to acquire and achieve. This will require a strategy in and of itself, as well as a degree of devotion that will show any potential mentor that you are coachable and ready to be a strong student.

Hiring a Mentor Versus Having One Choose You

In today's world, the value of a strong mentor is well-known. As such, an entire industry of hirable mentors have come up and made themselves available for people who are looking to learn more about their chosen industry, increase their confidence, build a better brand, or otherwise practice virtually any area of professional or personal self-development. For this reason, people now have the capacity to hire mentors if they desire. Choosing whether to hire a mentor versus whether to be chosen by one is a personal decision, but there are many things to consider when looking one way or the other. Let's take a look at the differences between the two.

Hirable mentors are easier to find and work with. They are actively looking for clients, meaning that they are willing to work with virtually anyone who is ready to pay them. This is a great system as it means you do not have to work as hard to be hired. However, it can also mean that your potential mentor is more focused on running a business and not necessarily the most qualified for the job. For that reason, you will need to qualify your mentor before hiring them. Another thing about hirable mentors is that they may or may not be the best at what they do, and they may or may not be actively involved in furthering their education and staying up to date on the relevant trends in their industry. Even though this is technically their job, not all mentors will do the same. There is nothing that actually regulates these mentors, so it will be up to you to make sure that they are qualified enough to actually mentor you. That being said, if you find a great one, getting the opportunity to work with them is significantly easier.

When it comes to getting chosen by a mentor, this particular choice is a great honor. If you are chosen by a great mentor, this means that they have chosen you above many others in your industry. They see potential and greatness in you, meaning their very choice in and of itself is a great vote of confidence toward your ability to become successful. Furthermore, they are doing the service out of the goodness of their heart, which means that they are there for more than just money. As a result, everything they teach you and share with you will be genuine and focused on your best interest. While hired mentors can certainly behave in the same way, there is always the tendency that they will not.

Choosing whether to hire a mentor or get chosen by one will depend on how hard you want to work to find and begin working with your mentor, how much money you have to invest (if you choose to hire one,) and who you resonate the most with. Sometimes, your desired mentor will actually be a professional mentor, meaning you will need budget to work with them anyway.

The Difference Between Mentors and Role Models

The next thing you need to understand is the difference between mentors and role models. The difference is quite significant, yet both are highly required to support you in generating professional and personal success in your life.

The key difference is that mentors are people that work directly with you and support you in creating success. Role models are people who may or may not even realize that you exist, but who inspired you to do your best in life. Typically, they embody the values that you have or are living the lifestyle that you are envisioning for yourself. This inspires you to emulate what they are doing so that you can create your own success in your own life. Having at least one role model is important because this supports you in having someone to look up to and something to aim toward. In essence, it gives a real edge to your dream, showing you in the flesh what it would look like for you to be where you desire to be.

In many cases, your role model and mentor will be one in the same. Being mentored by someone you look up to and whose success is something that you want to emulate in your life is actually one great way to begin qualifying potential mentors to make sure that you get the right one.

Where to Find a Mentor

Finding mentors is a three-step process. You must first research potential mentors, and then learn more about that mentor, then learn to get in touch with them in a way that earns you their respect. The first step, finding mentors, takes some time and patience.

The best way to find a mentor is to begin looking at your role models and discovering which one you would like to be coached by. In other words, which one do you like the most, who has the most similar life right now to the one that you desire to have? You should also consider who has the professional and personal achievements in their life that are akin to what you desire to create in your own life.

Once you have discovered a few people who you look up to the most, begin considering which one might be best at mentoring you. Pay attention to what they do, how their strategies are apparent in their work, the amount of success they are continuing to build, and how their personal lives look alongside their professional lives. The more you know, the better you will be able to determine if they share enough of your values to make working with that person worth your while.

The key now to finding your best mentor is deciding which of the few you have identified the best for you to work with is. The one that is the most aligned with who and what you desire to be in life, naturally, should be the best choice for you to pursue mentorship.

How to Qualify a Mentor

Qualifying a mentor is important. Above, we discussed many factors that would qualify a mentor for being one that is aligned enough with what you desire to support you in creating success. However, there are other things you need to qualify a mentor to make sure that they are worth your while as well.

Doing your research will support you in qualifying a mentor. You can do your research by first seeing if that person has ever mentored before. Some people may not be interested in mentoring at all, which may be apparent in their past actions or behavior. However, others may be extremely involved in or interested in mentorship.

You should also pay attention closely to how much your mentor is actually like you. If your mentor is too pushy, rather than just pushy enough to encourage you to do better or grow, or if they teach in a way that is too heavy-handed or not challenging enough for you, working with this mentor may not be the best fit.

Next, you need to consider their qualifications. This is especially true if you are planning on hiring a mentor. Far too many people in the industry call themselves mentors but are not nearly qualified enough to help you get anywhere in your own life. This can result in you unintentionally hiring an under or unqualified mentor if you are not careful. Many can be smooth talkers or have a tendency to swindle people into business with them under the idea that they are perfectly suited for the job. Be careful of this. You must always make sure that your mentor has professional qualifications or marks of success that prove that they are capable of teaching you what you desire to learn. You can easily qualify any mentor by seeing their credentials, looking at their professional milestones, and paying attention to their reputation in the online space. Someone who is genuinely qualified will have plenty of references and resources to show you that prove their ability, as well as an established presence that revolves around what they desire to teach you. The same goes for unpaid mentors, as well. If you are going to look for a mentor, make sure the mentor is qualified in what it is that you want to learn. For example, just because you are inspired by someone for their passion of family does not mean that they are going to be a great mentor for you in establishing a stronger brand and building your professional success as a financial advisor.

You need someone who is in your industry and who has qualifications in your industry to ensure that they truly are educated in a way that enables them to educate you.

Another thing you should look for in a mentor are references and testimonies. Pay attention to how other people perceive this person. Read through customer reviews, work-related reviews, and even testimonials or statements offered by those who have worked with this individual in the past. Take the time to get to know them and what supports them in making their judgment on this person. If an overwhelming number of people do not like this person or do not respond well to this person, working alongside them may not be the best idea.

Approaching Mentors

Once you have chosen and qualified a mentor, it is time to approach them. This is not a hugely necessary step in paid mentorships as most paid mentors are happily ready to take on anyone who is interested in paying. However, receiving the mentorship of an unpaid situation takes more planning, strategy, and intention. You need to earn the respect and appreciation of the potential mentor. The first thing you need to do is research this particular mentor to get to know more of who they are. The more you know about them, the easier it will be to talk to them as you will know what interests them, what they are passionate about, and what topics they are likely to want to share with you.

After you know what to talk about, contact the potential mentor. Make sure that you also have a reason for why you have chosen to contact them. This can be anything from being referred by a friend to seeing them at an event and wanting to communicate with them about that event. You want to create a reason for why you are reaching out and make it genuine. When they have contacted you back, then you can move on to the next step which is where you need to explain why you are getting in touch with the potential mentor. Make sure you are honest and clear about your reason for contacting them. Nothing will lose their respect faster than lying, being vague, or pretending you are attempting to contact them for any other reason and then spinning it around to attempt to get mentored by them.

If the potential mentor expresses interest in your request or says anything other than "no," you can begin sharing with them what your reasons for wanting a mentorship with them are. You can also let them know what your goals are. Letting them know exactly what it is that you are seeking, what areas you want to get support in, and what you hope to gain from the mentorship lets the potential mentor know what you are expecting. Then, they can determine if they are willing or not.

If the mentor agrees, the last step is to go ahead and set up your schedule to meet with the mentor and work with them. Make sure that you keep a consistent schedule and that you are always on time. Just because the mentor has agreed to work with you does not mean that they will never change their mind. Continue earning and maintaining the respect of your mentor by staying focused, taking action on what they educate you on, showing up for your interviews, and proving that you are actively engaged in the mentorship. They will not want to waste their time on someone who is not serious, so showing that you are serious is necessary. If you are not ready to concentrate and be mentored, consider waiting a bit longer before choosing to begin working with a mentor.

Chapter 11:
Monitoring Your Brand

The last step to having a successful brand is to know how to monitor your brand. Now that you know how to successfully build a brand, what goes into making and maintaining one, and how you can continue to grow your success, you need to know what it takes to monitor and encourage that success even further. Remember, as times change, trends will, too. The strategies in this book are great to get you started within the year of 2019, but new strategies, techniques, trends, and opportunities will inevitably be released and shared for marketers and companies to continue growing and sharing with their audience. Knowing how to stay on top of things will support you in staying on track and growing your brand for years to come.

Monitoring and maintaining your brand is going to revolve around five things: controlling your name, dealing with the negativity that rises, monitoring your analytics, refining your strategy, and dealing with your growth. These five topics will be the focus of this chapter.

Controlling Your Name

The first step in monitoring your brand is controlling your name. Now that you are building an identity for yourself, you need to be willing to keep your name under control. This means that any time someone searches for you, the content they find and what comes up is controlled and stays focused on promoting you and supporting you, not on tarnishing your name and resulting in you having to explain yourself or becoming a part of a scandal.

Controlling your name means that you have to be careful about how you engage in the online space. Make sure that you are always acting in alignment with your values and that you represent yourself to the best of your ability at all times. Any accidental or mistaken representations that are handled in a poor manner can easily be used against you, resulting in you having your entire reputation on the line for one poor experience. Always be cautious in how you behave online, and offline as well. As you grow to become more well-known, being caught doing less than ideal things in public and having that shared online can be just as damaging to your reputation.

You also need to search yourself online and see what comes up. If anything negative comes up about you, do your best to eliminate it. You can do so by reporting anything that breaks laws, asking the site owner to remove the content, or even burying the negativity with positive results. You can easily do this by fixating on creating many positive results so that everything that comes up about you is focused on the good.

Keeping your reputation focused on positive is necessary. If you want to refrain from having any misguided judgment passed on you for things you have done, you need to make sure that you are extremely cautious over your reputation. Even if your brand goes by a separate identity, your name is associated with it and this means that everything you say and do can be held against not only you but your brand as well. If you want to have a strong brand, you have to represent it strongly.

Dealing With Negativity

The next thing that you need to be prepared to do in your personal brand is to deal with negativity. All brands deal with negativity, but in a personal brand, negativity can feel especially harsh. Because you are your own brand, any negativity that floats around about you can feel very personal. This can be challenging to deal with. However, there are right and wrong ways to deal with negativity. It is essential that you deal with it correctly in order to refrain from tarnishing your name and reputation out of an attempt to protect yourself or stand up for yourself against someone who was being harsh or unkind toward you or your brand.

The first thing you need to know when dealing with negativity is that there is a very specific way *not* to deal with it. If dealt with it in the wrong way, negativity can turn into a major scandal or can have a massively damaging impact on your reputation. For example, you may accidentally reinforce someone's negative comment by fighting back or being a bully back to them. To you, you may simply be warding off someone that is mean. To the rest of the internet, it can look immature, unprofessional, and unkind.

It is essential that you never try to correct someone for how they are feeling about you or your content. This can look as though you are trying to control them or otherwise add fuel to the fire. In the end, this generally ends up in some form of fight or harsh criticism that escalates. In these circumstances, your best bet is to ignore or delete the comment.

If the negativity is offered as constructive criticism and not necessarily hate or harsh judgment being thrown about, handling it with a harsh hand can be unfair and unkind. Constructive criticism does not always feel nice to receive, but it is generally given with positive intentions. Recognizing this and taking the time to respond to these comments and thank them for their input is a great way to deal with it. Be careful not to mistake constructive criticism as a judgment or a mean comment because this can result in you attempting to defend yourself and a large fight breaking out over something that was intended to have constructive results. This can be a very embarrassing thing to endure, so avoiding it altogether by being level-headed and rational when reading and responding to feedback is always important.

What you should do whenever negativity comes up on your page is to truly just ignore it. Negativity is inevitable, especially as you grow. People love to share about how much they do not like things, many times, sharing in an extremely unkind manner. Engaging in these types of people or otherwise commenting back will only result in further fighting. Ignoring and deleting these comments is the best way. Instead of wasting your focus on harsh or unkind negativity, focus on those who support you and are cheering you on. They are more worth the focus and will not result in you handling a negative situation the wrong way and tarnishing your own reputation as a result.

Monitoring Analytics

Another mandatory method of monitoring your business is monitoring your analytics. You should have a set schedule for how frequently you are going to monitor your analytics. Then, pay attention to how each post and share has impacted your bottom line by way of engagement. Things that encouraged more followers, greater interaction and more engagement should be emulated and recreated or copied to continue creating great results. Things that do not perform well should be avoided in the future to prevent yourself from producing content that does not actually appeal to your audience.

Doing your analytics measuring over a week or even a month at a time will ensure that your results have time to accumulate. You do not want to check too frequently or you will not see the entirety of your results, as many things are seen for quite some time after being posted. Give your posts plenty of time to live out their lifespan so that you can get an accurate reflection of how they are performing and how your audience behaves in response to them. Furthermore, this will allow you to group together similar posts and compare them against other groups to see how they performed overall.

Your analytics are going to tell you how well your brand is performing and how well people are responding to you. Ideally, you want to continue monitoring your brand analytics across all social media platforms and other online platforms, such as your website, and use the information you received to support you in refining your strategy in going forward to keep it strong and successful. This will ensure that you are always growing forward, rather than stunting your growth or even reversing it by doing things that your followers do not particularly enjoy.

Refining Your Strategy

The results of your analytics are what will support you in refining your strategy. Your strategy should be refined to work in alignment with the trends shown in your analytics. So, sharing more of the content that performed well and less of what didn't is a great place to start. However, you want to get extremely specific. As you refine your strategy, look at specific aspects of your content that did and did not work well. Also, begin paying attention to the time that your posts have been most popular, and what methods of interaction your posts were engaged with most. These are the types of things that will show you how you can refine your strategy.

In addition to creating a refined strategy in response to your analytics, you also need to refine your strategy based on trends that are active in the social media industries. Pay attention to new features being introduced and always take advantage of them as soon as possible. At first, most new features get either a great response or a very poor response. However, over time, they level out and begin producing a consistent trend in their results. Recognizing and following these trends will not only help you refine your strategy, but they will also help you determine how you can use each feature to the best of its extent so that you can get the most out of it.

Lastly, make sure that you take a few minutes per week to actually search trending marketing strategies in your industry. This is going to support you in seeing what other people are doing, discovering what is working and what isn't, and inspire you to find new and more creative ways to share your brand. Following these industry trends will ensure that you are always on par with or ahead of the curve. That way, you can easily stay relevant in marketing and continue sharing with your audience in the ways that they respond to best.

Dealing With Your Growth

The last thing you need to pay attention to in monitoring your brand is dealing with your growth. As your growth continues to expand, you are going to need to know how to deal with the increasing engagement. Eventually, keeping up with all of the comments, messages, and other means of contact might be somewhat of a challenge. However, it is still just as necessary. Unless you are exceptionally large in the online space, with several hundreds of thousands of followers or even millions, most people are going to hope for and expect some form of acknowledgment or response from you. You want to actually respond as well because these are people who are supporting you, so responding is another way for you to maintain

153

your engagement and continue to earn their support. Furthermore, you do not want to miss over an important message that could be the start of a new deal, sale, or other opportunities for you. If you are not managing your growth well, you may miss over many opportunities.

Managing your growth is going to depend on how big you are getting. However, for the most part, as personal brands begin to grow larger, they will generally hire a virtual assistant or social media manager to keep an eye on things and maintain engagement. This is a great way to support you in making sure that all of the engagement is still earned. However, it may not be an option if you have personally branded under your own name. Having someone else commenting and engaging for you as you will not work, as this will take away from your authenticity and the integrity of your brand. Though, you might consider hiring a virtual assistant or social media manager and outwardly informing your followers and having them identify themselves in each comment and share to ensure that you are staying authentic and honest with your followers. This is a great way to receive the support of someone else without losing the trust of your followers.

Another great way to manage your growth is to begin scheduling a day each week or a few days each month to curate enough content to schedule for each platform. If done correctly, this can ensure that you have plenty of content to populate each platform for the duration of the month. Then, all you will need to do is update real-time updates as you feel like it and actively engage with those on your feed. This can reduce a lot of daily requirements, making it far easier to keep up with your platforms without feeling swamped.

Lastly, as you grow, you will likely find that you prefer one or two platforms to the rest. This will likely be the one that gets you the best results and keeps you most engaged with your audience.

While this does not mean you should completely abandon the others, it does mean that you can reduce the amount of time you spend on them and begin favoring the ones that are getting you the best results. This way, the other channels are still open, but you are not wasting time nurturing a platform that is not connecting you with your audience in the best way possible.

Conclusion

Thank you for reading *Personal Branding Secrets*!

This book was written to educate you on the secrets of creating success in your personal brand in the upcoming year, 2019. These relevant, modern, and trending techniques are all based on what is going to be the most popular next year. Everything you have learned was intended to show you how social media is changing and what you can do to take advantage of these changes and massively grow your personal brand, whether it is new or has been in existence for some time.

I hope that this book was able to introduce you to new, usable strategies in a way that supports you in putting them into effect in your own personal brand. From walking you through the process of building your vision and defining yourself apart from the rest of the crowd to highlighting the most important aspects of the four key social media platforms, I hope you were able to learn plenty to get you started and prepared once a new year starts.

Knowing how to run a successful personal brand requires a great deal of knowledge, but it also takes time, consistency, and devotion. Understand that by applying these techniques, you are not guaranteed to gain overnight success. Instead, you need to continue applying them and your success will grow over the course of the year.

The next step for you now is to create your strategy for 2019 and begin enforcing it right away. Even if you are reading this before 2019 officially arrives, getting a head start will only mean great things for your business. Make sure that as you go, you continue to refine your strategy and monitor your brand. The more you pay attention to how you are performing and how your reputation is developing, the easier it is for you to tweak it and create continued success in going forward. Be sure to check on your analytics at least once every couple of weeks to see how things are performing, and use this knowledge to continue growing.

Thank you!